W9-BWF-350

UNDERSTANDING MENTAL DISORDERS

What Is Self-Injury Disorder?

Other titles in the *Understanding Mental Disorders* series include:

What Is
Self-Injury
Disorder?

Janice M. Yuwiler

ReferencePoint
Press®

San Diego, CA

© 2016 ReferencePoint Press, Inc.
Printed in the United States

For more information, contact:
ReferencePoint Press, Inc.
PO Box 27779
San Diego, CA 92198
www.ReferencePointPress.com

LIBRARY OF CONGRESS CATALOGING-IN-PUBLICATION DATA

Yuwiler, Janice.
  What is self-injury disorder? / by Janice M. Yuwiler.
      pages cm. -- (Understanding mental disorders series)
   Audience: Grade 9 to 12.
   Includes bibliographical references and index.
   ISBN-13: 978-1-60152-928-2 (hardback)
   ISBN-10: 1-60152-928-7 (hardback)
   1. Self-mutilation--Juvenile literature. I. Title.
RJ506.S44Y89 2016
616.85'8200835--dc23
                                                              2015019621

CONTENTS

INTRODUCTION

The Hidden Epidemic

Self-injury is the act of purposefully injuring one's own body without the intent to commit suicide. It can include, among other things, cutting, burning, piercing, bruising, and breaking bones. Cutting, self-mutilation, self-injurious behavior, SI (for self-injury), nonsuicidal self-injury (NSSI), and self-harm are other terms used to describe the condition.

Self-injury is often associated with other mental health issues, including borderline personality disorder, depression, post-traumatic stress disorder (PTSD), and anxiety. However, people without other mental issues also self-injure. Self-injury is primarily used as a coping mechanism to deal with overwhelming emotions. In the words of one woman, "You don't feel like you're hurting yourself when you're cutting. You feel like this is the only way to take care of yourself."[1] Typically, those who self-injure lack healthy ways to cope with psychological pain caused by issues of personal identity, trauma, and/or difficulty finding one's place within the family or society.

The Hidden Epidemic

Self-injury has been around throughout the course of human history. Written accounts describe socially accepted self-mutilation. Examples include self-flagellation by Christian clergy seeking to rid themselves of sin, healers who injure themselves in order to heal others, rites of passage from childhood to adulthood, and the practice of enhancing one's beauty via scars and piercings.

But alongside injury that is socially accepted or religiously sanctioned, others have injured themselves in secret. Seeking relief from pain or struggling to feel alive, they have deliberately cut, burned, or struck themselves. They have hidden the bruises and scars, making up stories to explain their injuries if discovered.

In the mid-1800s psychiatrists began to publish case studies of people who self-injured. Typically, these cases were misidentified as unsuccessful suicides or viewed as symptoms of other mental health conditions. In 1938 psychiatrist Karl Menninger suggested that people who harmed themselves lacked the ability to tolerate overwhelming experiences and had trouble communicating their emotions to others. Menninger also attempted to sort self-mutilations into separate categories. But it was not until the work of psychiatrists Joel Kahan and E. Mansell Pattison in 1983 and psychiatrist Armando R. Favazza's book *Bodies Under Siege: Self-Mutilation in Culture and Psychiatry* in 1987 that self-injury gained recognition and acceptance as a diagnosis among the medical profession.

> "You don't feel like you're hurting yourself when you're cutting. You feel like this is the only way to take care of yourself."[1]
>
> —A female in her mid-twenties.

Further light was cast on the issue when, during an interview with the BBC in 1995, Princess Diana, a popular member of the British royal family, shared that she had cut herself numerous times, thrown herself down stairs, and deliberately fallen into a glass cabinet. Her disclosure brought public attention to the problem. In the early 2000s researchers all over the world began looking more closely at self-injury. In each country and culture studied, researchers found people who self-injure. According to Janis Whitlock, a researcher at Cornell University, "Self-injury is an overlooked public health issue. Far from being a fringe behavior, it was surprisingly common among the adolescents and young adults we surveyed."[2]

With research came new understanding, and in 2013 nonsuicidal self-injury was added to the fifth edition of the *Diagnostic and Statistical Manual of Mental Disorders* as a mental health disorder of its own, rather than merely a symptom of other mental health conditions. Self-injury is now recognized as one of the largest emerging mental health issues, but in many ways it remains hidden. There is still much that is not known about the disorder, including the full extent of the problem and how best to treat it. In addition, most people who self-injure keep it secret, injuring themselves in private and on parts of the

Britain's Princess Diana, pictured in 1997, publicly discussed her struggles with cutting and other types of self-injury. Her disclosure brought attention to the disorder.

body that can be hidden by clothing. Finally, the pain, the "badness," the fear, in other words, the reason someone self-injures—is internal, hidden from others; only the scars show on the outside what is hidden within.

Why Be Concerned?

Estimates of the number of people who self-injure continue to grow. The closer researchers look, the more widespread the problem appears. Self-injury is not just a problem among young people. Researchers are discovering that people of all ages and from all walks of life and cultures self-injure. Self-injury has now been documented throughout both the developed and developing world. In addressing the problem, there is no one medication or treatment that has been found to be effective. And there is no single reason people self-injure; the why and the how are as unique as the individual committing self-injury.

In addition, many people have an instinctive negative reaction to the idea of injuring oneself. Whitlock and her colleague Karen Rodham write, "The very nature of 'self-injury' defies deep instinctual human drives for self-preservation as well as strong social taboos related to self-inflicted injuries."[3] Many health professionals and mental and behavioral health therapists find themselves appalled by the injuries and unprepared to help those who self-injure. Their personal reactions can interfere with the delivery of appropriate treatment. Thus, those who seek treatment for self-injury often find themselves referred from one therapist to another.

With self-injury comes scars and the risk of disfigurement and disability. Even minor cuts and burns leave scars. When a knife cuts too deep, when bones shatter, or when individuals suffer a concussion or a severe burn, they can require hospitalization. Researchers at Georgia State University estimate that in 2007, approximately seventy-seven thousand injuries were treated in US emergency rooms for cutting and piercing, just two of many forms of self-injury. An accidentally cut tendon or a shattered bone can cause temporary or permanent disabilities, and cutting a major artery can cause death.

> "Self-injury is an overlooked public health issue. Far from being a fringe behavior, it was surprisingly common among the adolescents and young adults we surveyed."[2]
>
> —Janis Whitlock, a researcher at Cornell University.

Most experts agree that those who self-injure are struggling to survive and do not intend to kill themselves. However, self-injury and suicide share some of the same risk factors. In addition, it has been proposed that for those who self-injure, the existing pattern of injuring the body in times of stress can make it easier to commit suicide, compared to those who must first overcome a fear of hurting themselves.

Most people do not seek help for self-injury. A study published in the *Journal of American College Health* found that of 14,372 college students, close to a quarter of the students who self-injured said no one knew about their self-injury. Among those who had attended therapy for any reason, only 16.9 percent actually disclosed their self-injury to a health practitioner. In addition, experts note that as many as 30 percent of those who injure themselves more severely than expected do not seek medical treatment even if they think they need it.

The key to dealing with self-injury is to bring it out of the shadows and into the light. It is important not only to understand and address what is driving the need to self-injure but also to find healthier ways to cope with the stresses of life and any other underlying mental health issues.

CHAPTER 1

What Is Self-Injury?

Self-injury is the act of deliberately hurting oneself, but unlike suicide, there is no desire to stop living. In fact, it is just the opposite. Self-injury is often an attempt to survive, a way to cope with severe emotional pain. "Cutting is not attention seeking. It's not manipulative," explained a twenty-two-year-old male college student. "It's a coping mechanism—a punitive, unpleasant, potentially dangerous one—but it works. It helps me cope with strong emotions that I don't know how to deal with."[4]

Think of a young child who bangs his or her head or strikes out and hits things when frustrated. The impact stimulates the body and changes the way the child feels. Self-injury has been described as an extension of that desire to stimulate the body to feel different. Steven Jellá, a psychotherapist and associate executive director of San Diego Youth Services, says, "It can be helpful to think of self-injury as destroying one's tissue intentionally in order to feel different, without wanting to die."[5]

For many, self-injury involves using a knife, razor blade, broken glass, or other sharp object to cut, slash, scrape, pierce, or even carve words or symbols on the skin. Since this is the most commonly recognized form of self-injury, self-injury is often called "cutting." Other terms that refer to self-injury are self-mutilation, self-harm, self-injurious behavior, SI (for self-injury), deliberate self-harm, and nonsuicidal self-injury (NSSI).

Cutting is only one of the ways people self-injure. Cigarettes, matches, curling irons, and other hot objects can be used to burn the skin. Other people bang their heads, punch things or themselves, throw their bodies against the wall or other objects, pull out their hair, bite themselves, push objects such as pins and needles into their skin or insert them under the skin, pick at scabs to prevent healing, or break their bones. Those who self-injure can be incredibly creative about what they use to hurt themselves. Underlying all of the methods and actions is the fact that self-injury is used as a coping mechanism—an attempt to deal with emotional pain or to feel alive. "Self-injury may be desperate, but it is something I can *do*," says one young man. "For me it's a kind of hope, a way out. It's not giving up."[6]

What Self-Injury Is Not

Self-injury is typically *not* an attempt to change one's body. Throughout history people have changed or injured their bodies in the pursuit of health and beauty or as part of religious practice. Examples are male circumcision, pierced ears, tattoos, and scarring as a rite of passage into adulthood. These injuries are, for the most part, socially acceptable and have cultural meaning. The pain that comes with getting a tattoo or piercing is tolerated because of the desired end result. So although the body is deliberately injured, these practices are typically not considered self-injury.

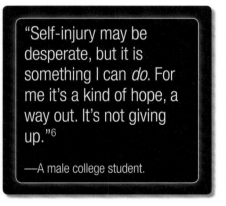

"Self-injury may be desperate, but it is something I can *do*. For me it's a kind of hope, a way out. It's not giving up."[6]

—A male college student.

That said, there are some who consider any form of destroying the body's tissue self-injury. They point to those who undergo frequent plastic surgery or extreme tattooing or piercing and wonder if some of that behavior is simply paying someone else to do the harm. In other words, certain people may use plastic surgery, tattooing, and/or piercing as a way to make their body feel different without the stigma attached to deliberately hurting oneself. In her memoir, *Comes the Darkness, Comes the Light*, Vanessa Vega discusses how she subjected herself to medical experiments at the local medical school. "I rationalized that if I wasn't doing the cutting, and it benefited society, then it wasn't really self-injury. I was donating plasma twice a week at the local blood bank and whole blood every two months. . . . A finger stick. A muscle biopsy. *Anything* to feel I had control over the pain in my life. Anything to keep the pain from the past from catching up to me."[7]

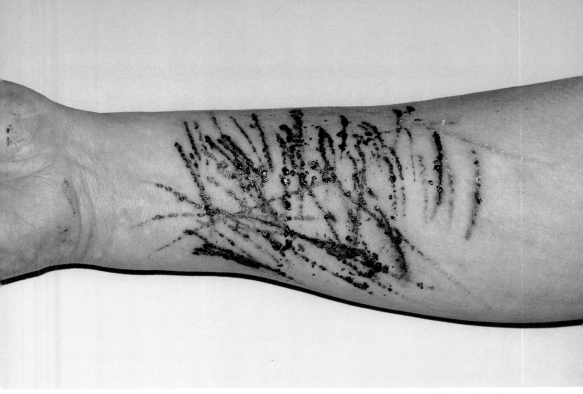

Self-inflicted lacerations leave bright red scars—a vivid reminder of the patient's inner struggles. Knives, razor blades, broken glass, or other sharp objects may be used to cut, slash, or pierce the skin.

As more research is done, experts might be better able to determine when socially accepted injuries such as tattooing, piercing, plastic surgery, and even starting fights constitute self-injury.

Self-Injury Is Not a Suicide Attempt

For many years it was assumed that self-injuries were unsuccessful suicide attempts. Now experts understand that self-injury and suicide are different things. Typically, individuals commit suicide because they can no longer bear the pain of living or because they believe they are a burden on others. Either way, the goal is to die. This is the opposite of self-injury. Experts agree that those who self-injure do not typically intend to end their lives. Rather, self-injury is used as a way to relieve pain or frustration, as a form of self-punishment, or as a way to control at least a portion of one's own life. It is also used to create sensation strong enough to end the psychological numbness the person might be feeling. All of these, at their core, are attempts to cope and go on living.

Why Is It So Hard to Measure How Many Teens Self-Injure?

Estimates of the number of teens who self-injure range from 13 percent to 45 percent; a very large range. There is a big difference between fewer than one out of every five teens and almost half of all teens self-injuring. Part of the reason these estimates vary so much is because early research was done with small groups of people—what are known as small sample sizes. Sample size is important when doing research; if only a few people are studied, there is a greater chance to produce data that does not reflect the population as a whole and to have numbers that vary widely between studies.

In addition, researchers sometimes measure different things. For example, some studies looked at self-injury among students in middle school and others among students in high school or college. Still others studied teens hospitalized for mental health issues, whereas others studied teens in the community, which affects their findings. In general, researchers find higher self-injury rates among teens with other mental health issues and in studies that define self-injury more broadly. Rates are two to three times higher when a checklist of behaviors is used versus a single question. Higher rates are also found among those returning questionnaires versus those who are interviewed in person. This difference in estimates is common in new fields of study, where the definitions are still being discussed and common measurement tools have not yet been developed.

Occasionally things will go terribly wrong when a person self-injures. The self-injury will be more severe than intended, and the person will die from his or her injuries. Despite this, those who self-injure are quite clear that death is not the intent of their self-injury. As psychologists Judy A. Stone and Shari M. Sias explain, "Clients are generally aware of the fine line they walk between self-injury and suicide and are resentful of doctors and mental health professionals who mistake their self-harm as suicide attempts."[8]

The difference between self-injury and suicide is underscored by the different methods used. Patrick L. Kerr of West Virginia University School of Medicine notes that most suicides involve self-inflicted gunshots, hanging, overdose and/or self-poisoning, or jumping from lethal heights. Only 2 percent of suicides are due to cutting. The methods used most in non-fatal suicide attempts also differ from the common methods used for self-injury. The majority of non-fatal suicide attempts involve drug overdoses. This is in direct contrast with the methods used for self-injury. Approximately 70 percent of those who self-injure report that they cut themselves.

How Many Are Affected?

Although people have self-injured throughout history, the study of self-injury is relatively new. There is still much to be understood, including the scope of the problem. Estimates of the number of people who self-injure vary widely, depending on the population studied and how *self-injury* is defined. This has been a continuing problem because without knowing how many people self-injure and under what circumstances, it is hard to know what to do to address the problem.

Since the late 1990s a number of researchers have set out to better understand the extent of the problem. One of the larger studies that looked at the number of people who self-injure—also called the prevalence of self-injury—was conducted by Janis Whitlock and her colleagues at Cornell University. Of the 11,529 students they surveyed at eight colleges in the Northeast and Midwest, 15.3 percent reported a history of self-injury, and 6.8 percent had self-injured within the previous year. Other studies have had similar results.

> "Clients are generally aware of the fine line they walk between self-injury and suicide and are resentful of doctors and mental health professionals who mistake their self-harm as suicide attempts."[8]
>
> —Psychologists Judy A. Stone and Shari M. Sias.

Looking across many of the studies to date, the best estimate seems to be that among adolescents, 15 percent to 28 percent self-injure. That is roughly one in five young people. However, it is not just young people who self-injure. Experts estimate that 4 percent to 6 percent of the adult population self-injures as well. E. David Klonsky at the University of British Columbia studied adults and found the "lifetime prevalence of [self-injury] was 5.9 %, including 2.7 % who had self-injured five or more times."[9]

Who Self-Injures

Researchers and people who treat those who self-injure are beginning to see patterns emerge regarding who is most likely to self-injure. They have found that both males and females self-injure and that adolescents have the highest risk for self-injury. Many studies report that females self-injure at a higher rate than males. Research studies also suggest that males and females tend to use different methods of self-injury. A 2012 study by Andrea L. Barrocas and her colleagues at the University of Denver found that "girls reported cutting and carving of the skin most often, whereas boys reported hitting themselves most often."[10] One reason studies have found that females are more likely to self-injure than males may be due to the questions asked and the type of injuries studied. Most studies have asked about a person's experience with cutting, which is a type of injury more common among females than males. As studies ask questions about other types of self-injury, there is evidence that male self-injury may be more common than thought. A number of recent studies have found no difference in the rates of self-injury for males and females.

For the most part, researchers have found that people of all races, ethnicities, and education and income levels engage in self-injury. In addition, the percentage of adolescents who self-injure in the United States is similar to the percentage of adolescents who self-injure in other developed countries. "Perhaps the most salient theme to emerge from existing literature is that there is no one profile for an individual who self-injures,"[11] report Janis Whitlock and Karen Rodham of the University of Bath in England. That said, people liv-

"Perhaps the most salient theme to emerge from existing literature is that there is no one profile for an individual who self-injures."[11]

—Researchers Janis Whitlock and Karen Rodham.

Methods of Self-Injury by Gender

According to a study of 665 young people between the ages of seven and sixteen, both boys and girls self-injure by cutting or carving their skin, burning, and hitting themselves. Among girls the most common forms of self-injury are cutting and carving of the skin. Among boys the most widespread form of self-injury is to hit themselves.

Rates	Lifetime	Cut/carve skin	Burn skin	Insert objects	Pick skin	Hit self	Other
Overall	8%	45.3%	13.2%	15.1%	7.5%	47.2%	18.9%
Girls	9%	63.6%	18.2%	15.2%	9.1%	42.4%	15.2%
Boys	6.7%	15%	5%	15%	5%	55%	25%

Note: Percentages do not add up to 100 percent because youth reported multiple methods.

Source: A.L. Barrocas, et al., "Rates of Nonsuicidal Self-Injury in Youth: Age, Sex and Behavioral Methods in a Community Sample," *Pediatrics*, July 2012. www.ncbi.nlm.gov.

ing with mental health issues are more likely to self-injure, including people with borderline personality disorder, depression, dissociation, and eating disorders. Researchers have found that among people receiving psychotherapy, those who self-injure tend to report high levels of depression and anxiety and comparatively few coping mechanisms.

In her book *A Bright Red Scream: Self-Mutilation and the Language of Pain*, Marilee Strong notes there is another group that self-injures. They are "often bright, talented, and creative achievers—perfectionists who push themselves beyond all human bounds, people-pleasers who cover their pain with a happy face."[12] Studies are finding that self-injury is more common than expected among people who are high-functioning with no exposure to trauma, and these people are the mostly likely to go undetected and without treatment.

When Do People Start to Self-Injure?

Studies have found that children as young as age seven engage in self-injury. Professor Benjamin Hankin of the University of Denver and Professor John Abela of Rutgers University studied a group of young people over time and found that only 8 percent of the students (then eleven to fourteen years old) self-injured at the start of the study, but two and half years later, 18 percent reported they self-injured. Their findings match much of the research to date that shows self-injury frequently starts in early adolescence when teens are emotionally volatile and face increasing peer pressure, loneliness, and conflicts with parents and authority figures.

Researchers have found that the majority of people begin to self-injure either between the ages of thirteen to fifteen, or in their late teens when they are of college age, and that self-injury tends to de-

Boosting

Athletes with spinal cord injuries have used self-injury in an effort to increase their athletic performance. Because the bodies of those paralyzed below the waist may not control blood pressure and heart rate well, the body of a paraplegic athlete may not respond as needed to the demands of intense physical activity, causing the athlete to tire more quickly. Lacking feeling in their legs and lower body, some athletes have intentionally broken a bone, used electric shocks, or caused stress to their lower body to boost their blood pressure and heart rate, which increases the body's use of oxygen and has been shown to enhance athletic performance.

Called "boosting," this practice can be dangerous. It increases the risk for stroke, heart attacks, seizures, bleeding in the brain, and vision problems. Boosting was banned by the International Paralympic Committee in 1994. However, a survey conducted by the committee during the 2008 Paralympic games found that of the ninety-nine athletes who responded, 16.7 percent indicated they had tried boosting in training or competition. Like other doping checks, parathletes are now checked for continuously elevated blood pressure, and athletes who test positive are barred from competition.

cline in early adulthood. About 25 percent try it once and never self-injure again. There is research to suggest that most people self-injure less than ten times in their lifetime, and a majority stop within the first six months. However, for about 20 percent of those who self-injure, the behavior becomes a habit that becomes increasingly difficult to stop. Although the number of methods used and the frequency may increase the longer someone self-injures, people who report they have self-injured, even if only one time, report moderate to severe tissue damage.

Of the 15 percent to 20 percent of high schoolers who were found to self-injure in a study by Lindsay A. Taliaferro and her colleagues, more than a quarter self-injured about once a week. This is consistent with other results. Matthew K. Nock of Harvard University found that teens he surveyed reported having thought about engaging in self-injury approximately five times a week and had self-injured once or twice a week.

The first time someone self-injures, it is often by chance. Typically, the person will have been struggling, feeling unhappy, isolated, or bad, and then something happens that makes the person feel even worse—a fight or argument, or another sort of trigger. People describe being in that situation and seeing a scissors, a knife, or a lighter and just picking it up and using it to hurt themselves. Over time, what was initially an impulsive act can become a compulsion. For some people, especially those who are struggling with other mental health conditions, self-injury can become an ingrained coping mechanism that is hard to give up.

Relationship to Other Mental Health Issues

For a long time self-injury was thought to be a symptom of other mental health disorders. For example, since as many as 70 percent to 75 percent of those with borderline personality disorder self-injure, self-injury is one of the nine symptoms used to diagnose borderline personality disorder. Self-injury is also associated with other mental health conditions. Approximately 69 percent of those with dissociation and dissociative disorders—those who feel psychologically and/or physically removed from reality—self-injure. So do approximately 42 percent of those with major depression. Although experts now agree that self-injury can exist as a separate disorder, it is found in about 40 percent to 60 percent of adolescents and 19 percent to 25 percent of adults who live with other mental health issues. This is three to four times the prevalence of self-injury reported in surveys of students and adults who have not been diagnosed with other mental health conditions.

There are a variety of risk-taking behaviors in which struggling teens may choose to engage. Nock and colleagues' 2009 study reports "that when self-injurious thoughts occur, adolescents report simultaneously having thoughts of using drugs or alcohol and of engaging in bingeing and purging approximately 15–35% of the time, suggesting that these behaviors may represent different forms of behavior that serve the same function."[13] This connection might explain the association experts have seen between self-injury and eating disorders, with between 27 percent and 55 percent of those who live with anorexia also self-injuring. As Vega, who struggled with an eating disorder as well as self-injury, wrote in her memoir:

> It is like my body and mind can only focus on one thing at a time: feelings or weight. If I am obsessed with my weight, then it seems like I am able to shut off many of the feelings that contribute to self-injury. But if my eating disorder is under control, I start to fear getting fat, become even more insecure, and before I know it, I will go from cutting only once a month or so to cutting multiple times a week.[14]

Relationship of Self-Injury to Suicide

Self-injury and suicide are two different things, but there is a relationship between them. Researchers have found that those who self-injure are thirty to forty times more likely to commit suicide at some point than those who do not self-injure. Whitlock's 2011 study of 11,529 college students found that those who self-injure more frequently and/or use more severe methods to self-injure are at greater

Research suggests that people who self-injure are more likely to contemplate or attempt suicide than those who do not. Depression, binge drinking, and a history of abuse are common risk factors for both suicide and self-injury.

risk for suicide. Other studies have found that among high school and college students, 35 percent to 45 percent of students who self-injure have also thought about suicide.

Looking to better understand the relationship between self-injury and suicide, in 2012 researchers at Georgia State University found that self-injury and suicide share some of the same risk factors; These include depression, binge drinking, weapon carrying, having been abused, and impulsivity. In particular, young people who report they self-injure and attempt suicide are likely to be impulsive, have little parental support, and have a history of being abused. These issues are less common in young people who self-injure but have never tried to commit suicide or young people who have attempted suicide but never self-injured. Another study published in *Academic Pediatrics* in 2012 found that having a mental health problem and running away from home were also factors, but that "hopelessness constituted the leading factor to increase the likelihood that youth who self-injured also attempted suicide."[15]

Classifications of Self-Injury

As researchers and therapists seek to understand and treat self-injury, a number of classification systems have been proposed. One system, developed by Armando R. Favazza of the University of Missouri and Richard Rosenthal of Columbia University, along with psychiatrist Daphne Simeon, groups together different patterns of self-injury into more easily understood categories. These include:

Superficial or moderate self-mutilation. This is the most common form of self-injury. It is found throughout the world and includes self-injuries that are typically of mild to moderate severity. It most commonly begins in adolescence. This category is further divided into three subtypes:

- *Compulsive* self-injury, which tends to occur many times a day and is the most repetitive and ritualistic of the three subtypes. For example, pulling hair out one strand at a time from a specific spot on the scalp, eyebrows, arm, or leg; or scratching or picking at real or imaginary wounds or skin lesions. These behaviors appear to be more subconscious than other forms of self-injury and seem to operate more like an obsessive-compulsive disorder.

- *Episodic* self-injury, which occurs every so often. It typically involves an isolated number of incidents throughout an individual's life and often occurs in response to stress or life events. Cutting, burning, needle sticking, bone breaking, and self-hitting are among the methods used. Cutting appears to be the most common method, followed by burning and self-hitting.

- *Repetitive* self-injury, which includes skin cutting, burning, needle sticking, bone breaking, and interference with wound healing; the same methods used in episodic self-injury. The difference is that instead of the behavior being a short-term coping mechanism, the behavior has evolved into a preoccupation that is repeated over and over. After a while, it assumes a life of its own and becomes part of the individual's identity. For example, someone who identifies herself as a "cutter" and describes herself as "addicted" to self-injury would fit into this category.

Stereotypic self-mutilation. This includes monotonous, repetitive acts such as head banging, self-biting, hair pulling, chewing on fingers, and pressing on one's eyeballs. It can occur both in private and in the company of others. This form of self-injury seems to be closely tied to biological problems with the brain. It is most commonly seen among those with developmental disabilities or specific neurological and psychiatric disorders, including autism, Rett syndrome, Tourette's syndrome, Cornelia de Lange syndrome, and Lesch-Nyhan syndrome. The acts tend to follow a fixed pattern and are often rhythmic.

Major self-mutilation. This is the rarest form of self-injury. It is defined as infrequent acts of severe self-injury in which a significant amount of body tissue is destroyed; for example, amputation of a limb, gouging out an eye, or castration. This type of self-injury is most commonly committed by those suffering from acute psychosis. The most common reasons given for committing major self-injury are typically associated with religion, demonic influences, or guilt over sexual thoughts and activities.

A Disorder of Its Own

All research points to self-injury as a mental health condition that occurs independently of other mental health issues and is distinctly different from suicide. The directors of S.A.F.E. (Self Abuse Finally Ends) Alternatives summarize it well in their definition of self-injury as "the deliberate mutilation of the body or body part, not with the intent to commit suicide but as a way of managing emotions that seem too painful for words to express."[16]

CHAPTER 2

Why Do People Self-Injure?

There is no single or simple reason why people self-injure. Typically, self-injury is the result of an inability to cope in healthy ways with psychological pain. In general, those who self-injure have a hard time controlling, expressing, or understanding emotions, but the mix of emotions that trigger self-injury are complex. When, how, and why someone self-injures are as unique as the individual person.

Approximately half of those who self-injure are victims of physical, sexual, or verbal abuse or have suffered the loss of a parent through death or divorce when they were a child. Many of those who self-injure struggle with other mental issues or an eating disorder. In addition, many people who use self-injury tend to be impulsive. There is still a great deal of research to be done before the causes of self-injury are well understood, but it appears that most people self-injure to change the way they feel. According to experts, the vast majority of explanations for self-injury are functional. That is, self-injury helps the person cope with and manage situations or feelings.

Researchers are finding that although the reasons people first try self-injury vary, social motivations (such as to communicate distress or to identify with a group) and impulse are the most common reasons people try self-injury. The reasons for continuing to self-injure are different. Most people continue to self-injure because it helps them deal with uncomfortable feelings, stress, emotional or physical pain, frustration, and anger, or just to feel something, anything at all.

Self-Injury as an Attempt to Cope

Matthew K. Nock of Harvard University notes, "Self-injury is performed in most cases as a means of self-soothing or of help-seeking."[17]

Indeed, people who self-injure describe being overwhelmed by emotion and desperately needing a way to release or banish the feelings that threaten to drown them. One fifteen-year-old can attest to this. "When I'm self-injuring, I want to relieve emotional pain and keep on living," she said. "Self-injury helps me get through the moment."[18]

"The mix of emotions that triggers self-injury is complex," note experts at the Mayo Clinic. "For instance, there may be feelings of worthlessness, loneliness, panic, anger, guilt, rejection, self-hatred or confused sexuality."[19] It is not the specific feeling that matters so much as the fact that the feelings are intense and difficult to deal with.

> "When I'm self-injuring, I want to relieve emotional pain and keep on living. . . . Self-injury helps me get through the moment."[18]
>
> —A fifteen-year-old female.

Marilee Strong, author of *A Bright Red Scream: Self-Mutilation and the Language of Pain*, has interviewed many people who are self-injurers. She agrees that people typically self-injure because they have no other outlet for their pain. "People cut and burned and bashed their bodies precisely because they could not put into words the pain and confusion they were feeling inside themselves," she says. "Instead of discharging negative emotions verbally, they had to do so physically."[20]

The feelings of one young woman exemplify this. She recalls:

I started to feel frightened of nothing in particular. I wanted the fear to go away. I tried to tell myself that there was nothing wrong. School was okay. . . . But the fear wouldn't go away. I banged my forehead against the wall of my bedroom. My head stung, but only for a moment. . . . I knew I needed something that would last much longer. It had to last so long that by the time it went away, my feeling of dread would be gone and wouldn't come back, at least for a long time.[21]

This young woman decided to cut herself. She explains, "It wasn't pain I was feeling, it was like an injection of Novocaine that the dentist uses; it makes pain go away even though the needle 'pricks' as the

Top Reasons for Self-Injuring

The initial reason for trying self-injury tends to be social, such as being angry at oneself or someone else, or hoping someone will notice something is wrong. However, those who self-injure more than once typically do so to manage or cope with their emotions.

Initial Motivations for and the Functions of Repeated Self-Injury

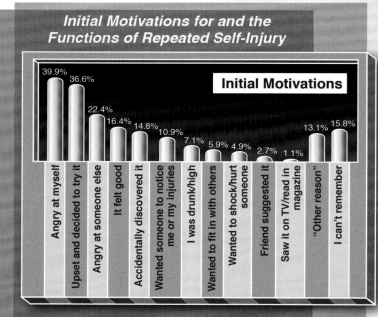

Initial Motivations

Reason	Percent
Angry at myself	39.9%
Upset and decided to try it	36.6%
Angry at someone else	22.4%
It felt good	16.4%
Accidentally discovered it	14.8%
Wanted someone to notice me or my injuries	10.9%
I was drunk/high	7.1%
Wanted to fit in with others	5.9%
Wanted to shock/hurt someone	4.9%
Friend suggested it	2.7%
Saw it on TV/read in magazine	1.1%
"Other reason"	13.1%
I can't remember	15.8%

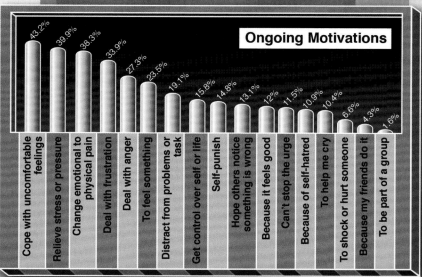

Ongoing Motivations

Reason	Percent
Cope with uncomfortable feelings	43.2%
Relieve stress or pressure	39.9%
Change emotional to physical pain	38.3%
Deal with frustration	33.9%
Deal with anger	27.3%
To feel something	23.5%
Distract from problems or task	19.1%
Get control over self or life	15.8%
Self-punish	14.8%
Hope others notice something is wrong	13.1%
Because it feels good	12%
Can't stop the urge	11.5%
Because of self-hatred	10.9%
To help me cry	10.4%
To shock or hurt someone	6.6%
Because my friends do it	4.3%
To be part of a group	1.6%

Note: Percentages do not add up to 100 percent because respondents could report more than one reason.

Source: Jennifer Muehlenkamp, et al. The American Association of Suicidology, "Interpersonal Features and Functions of Nonsuicidal Self-Injury," *Suicide and Life-Threatening Behavior*, February 13, 2013.

dentist puts it in. And because I controlled the pain, there was no fear with it." She goes on to describe watching her blood flow across her forearm and recalls, "That was enough for me to see. The fear and dread were gone. . . . It was like medicine for my fears."[22]

This young woman is not alone. In a study cited in the *Journal of Youth and Adolescence* of 240 females who habitually self-injured, 79 percent reported that they self-injured to control their mind and stop it from racing, and 65 percent reported self-injuring to feel relaxed. "The whole idea of cutting yourself is ironic," says a sixteen-year-old female. "Making yourself hurt to feel better is a really wicked and deranged thing. But to me, it's normal."[23]

> "The mix of emotions that triggers self-injury is complex. For instance, there may be feelings of worthlessness, loneliness, panic, anger, guilt, rejection, self-hatred or confused sexuality."[19]
>
> —Mayo Clinic staff.

A series of studies conducted by Harvard researchers between 2006 and 2008 found that people who self-injure have a stronger physiological response to a frustrating task or stressful event than those who do not self-injure. They may have to work harder to stop bad thoughts and feelings and may have less ability to tolerate stress. In addition, they tend to have more trouble communicating their feelings verbally and tend to have fewer problem-solving skills in social situations.

Physiologically, the release of endorphins into the bloodstream after an injury both reduces pain and leads to a feeling of well-being. This is an adaptive response on the part of the body that allows someone to escape after being attacked or injured. In the case of self-injury, it may be that the release of endorphins calms the stress of the emotions that trigger the self-injury. There is some evidence that those who are exposed to repeated shock or injury (such as that experienced with child abuse) may become used to the endorphins the body produces in response to pain. When times are calm and the endorphins are not needed, the person may experience withdrawal and feelings of tension and discomfort. Self-injury may serve to bring the endorphin levels back to what the person is used to and bring relief from the discomfort of withdrawal.

Self-Injury as an Act of Control

Some people are forced to deal with problems that are beyond their control. An alcoholic or depressed mother, an abusive father, the death of a loved one, bullying at school, intense pressure to perform athletically or academically, or the need to be strong for others in the face of an unstable environment may cause some individuals to turn to the one thing they can control: their body. In the words of one young woman as she recalled a time in her life when she self-injured, "I was just so engulfed in the pain of others that I had no idea how to deal with overwhelming emotional stimulants. I had a really hard time understanding that my problems were environmental. I thought I was an angry person. And my answer to anything that was over-whelming was to cut."[24]

Self-injury can often be ritualistic; it may follow a specific pattern that the individual controls, in contrast to other aspects of life that may feel out of control. Gathering the tools, sterilizing them, laying out the antiseptic to clean the wound and the bandages to protect it—some people who self-injure find such routines offer them pre-dictability and a degree of comfort. The injuries themselves may be precisely inflicted and a certain length, size, or pattern. Care of the in-juries may allow the individuals to comfort and care for themselves in a way no one around them is doing. Self-injury can be a way of exert-ing control by focusing inward when it is too dangerous or impossible to control the external situation. As Vega describes in her memoir, "I want to have some control, any control, over [what] is happening in my life and so I take some. I take control in one of the few ways I know how. I hurt myself."[25]

Self-Injury to Cope with Dissociation and Feel Alive

About half of those who self-injure are survivors of child abuse, trau-ma, or sexual abuse. Moya Alfonso and Robert F. Dedrick of the Uni-versity of South Florida note that for those receiving help for mental health issues, "sexual abuse has been identified as the single best pre-dictor of self-injury."[26]

Survivors of abuse and other forms of trauma may cope by dis-sociating from their bodies. In other words, they may purposefully

When outside pressures become too much to endure, some young people turn to self-injury in an effort to take control of their lives. Living with abuse or bullying or even feeling extreme pressure to perform athletically or academically can boil over into unhealthy practices such as cutting.

or unconsciously "remove" themselves from the situation. This has been described as feeling like they are watching themselves in a movie rather than being present during the abuse. Some dissociate so completely they are unable to remember the details of what happened. Others deaden their emotions because it is too painful to feel or remember the trauma they endured.

Those who have deadened their emotions to survive can feel like they are just going through the motions of living. The pain of self-injury and the sight of blood can break through the dissociation and allow the person to feel alive and part of the world, at least for a while. "The infliction of pain, and the drawing of blood, is an effort at feeling, being alive, and delineating boundaries,"[27] explains Dr. Brian Daniel Smith of Michigan State University. "Pain and blood were proof that I was alive and hurting,"[28] remembers one woman of her experience cutting when she was a teen.

Self-Injury as Self-Punishment

Survivors of child abuse, sexual abuse, or bullying, as well as those who are struggling with their sexuality or feelings of worthlessness, may blame themselves and use self-injury to punish themselves for "bad" behavior. They may believe that the abuse is their fault or is due to something they did or something they lack. Survivors of abuse may not realize that their abuser is responsible for the abuse, not them. Other people may be unable to accept themselves as different from others around them and feel the difference is their fault. "I hurt so badly on the inside for the person I wanted to be and others expected me to be," recalls Vanessa Vega. "But in the end, I was only me and it never seemed good enough . . . and so I sought out a way to punish myself because that's what I thought I deserved."[29]

> "The infliction of pain, and the drawing of blood, is an effort at feeling, being alive, and delineating boundaries."[27]
>
> —Psychiatrist Brian Daniel Smith.

The belief that they are to blame is evident in words like *failure*, *loser*, or *disgrace* that some people who self-injure have carved into their skin.

In fact, those who self-injure report much higher levels of self-criticism than those who do not. In some studies about half of those who self-injure report feeling self-hatred and self-anger immediately prior to self-injuring. "The presence of a self-punitive or self-critical style may emerge as a result of depression and/or could be the result of earlier abuse or criticism from others," notes Nock. It can cause a person to "learn to respond to perceived failures with self-criticism and ultimately 'self-abuse' in the form of self-injury."[30]

Self-Injury as a Call for Help

Although most people who self-injure do so in private and try to hide what they are doing, some will use self-injury as a cry for help.

Link to Neurobiological Imbalances

Neurotransmitters are the chemicals that control communication between cells in the brain. They have become the focus of research because they seem to hold the key to understanding behavior and emotions. The following neurotransmitters appear to be involved in self-injury.

- **Serotonin.** This is a neurotransmitter that affects mood and aggression. There is evidence linking decreased serotonin levels with self-injury and many of the other mental health issues with which self-injury is associated, including depression, obsessive-compulsive disorder, and impulsivity.

- **Endorphins.** Endorphins are chemicals produced by the brain to reduce pain. Many of those who self-injure report feeling little to no pain. It has been suggested that those who were abused during childhood may have become used to high levels of endorphins, which function like morphine in the brain to decrease pain. When stressed, these people have even higher pain thresholds. It has also been proposed that individuals who have experienced trauma and abuse may have become used to high levels of endorphins and self-injure when those levels drop.

- **Dopamine.** Dopamine is one of the stress hormones. There is evidence linking dopamine sensitivity to self-injury, especially among individuals with Lesch-Nyhan syndrome and Tourette's syndrome, which are both tied to organic problems with the brain and self-injury.

Britain's Princess Diana, mother of Prince William, once shared that she cut herself in front of her husband, Prince Charles, to get him to recognize the pain she was in. "You have so much pain inside yourself that you try and hurt yourself on the outside because you want help,"[31] she once told Martin Bashir, a reporter at the BBC.

There is evidence that behavior can serve as an effective means of communication when language is absent or ineffective. Just think of the average two- or three-year-old who wants something but has few ways to tell others what it is.

Self-injury, too, can develop out of a need to get others to listen or a need to increase the impact of communication. For example, a teen-age boy may respond to teasing by first ignoring it, then by asking his tormentors to stop—perhaps at first politely and then more forcefully.

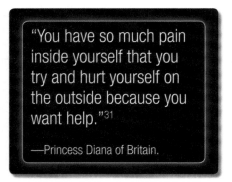

"You have so much pain inside yourself that you try and hurt yourself on the outside because you want help."[31]

—Princess Diana of Britain.

When that fails to work, he might start dressing in a way that makes him look more threatening, such as dark cloth-ing and studs. He may eventually turn to self-injury as a display of strength or resilience or to get the attention of someone who might help.

Research presented in the *Annual Review of Clinical Psychology* suggests that those who self-injure have more trouble finding the right words and expressing their emotions than those who do not self-injure, as well as fewer social problem–solving skills. "It is easier and more comfortable to pierce her skin and draw blood than to confront the people and emotions that anguish her,"[32] says psychologist Karen Conterio of a sixteen-year-old female patient. Another sixteen-year-old female thousands of miles away expresses the same feelings. "Scars and blood say more for me than words ever could." She goes on to say, "I hate confrontation, and I can never fight back because my greatest fear is being abandoned by the people I care about. Now whenever my parents yell at me, I start shaking. I go into my room, close the door and frantically go about raising blood drops on my skin until I feel calm again."[33]

In addition, a 2007 study suggests that the families of those who self-injure tend to show higher levels of hostility and criticism. This may make it harder for weak verbal communication to be heard.

Self-Injury in Groups

Infrequent but growing, especially among males, is self-injury done with a group. This sometimes takes the form of a challenge game—for example, a contest to see who can take the most punches or hold their arm over a flame the longest. Self-injury among peers can also be an attempt to seek social connection or attention in some way. The hunger for connections and bonding with similarly alienated people may explain the "cutting epidemics" seen on adolescent psychiatric wards. In such epidemics, those who have never before self-injured begin to do so in public or private, seemingly in an attempt to establish kinship with others. A group psychology may develop in which members share each other's highs, rescue each other from their lows, and collectively find relief by releasing strong feelings through self-injury.

Self-injury in a group can also introduce young people to self-injury, and encourage them to hurt themselves on their own. For example, a teen who was introduced to self-injury during a "game" may notice that self-injury felt good in an odd way. Perhaps it calmed the anxious feelings with which he was struggling. He may seek out more of these "games," and gradually move on to injuring himself in private.

Self-Injury and Social Contagion

The use of self-injury is growing among today's teens, and many experts think contagion has played a role. Contagion is the idea that a behavior or act becomes more popular with exposure. Indeed, there are an increasing number of media stories about self-injury, including those that feature celebrities who share stories of their personal struggles with self-injury. Self-injury themes also increasingly appear in music and books, and the topic is often the subject of chat rooms, blogs, and message boards. This has raised young people's awareness of the issue—and not necessarily in a positive way. For example, a study reported in the *American Journal of Health Education* found that 46.8 percent of middle school students surveyed knew of a friend who had self-injured. In addition, students who knew a friend had self-injured were more likely to have tried self-injury themselves.

Other researchers have noticed that self-injury can move through a population, or even cluster in certain populations, in very much the same way a bacteria or virus would. Teens who are particularly sensitive to their peers; those who are struggling to establish meaningful relationships; and those who yearn to be accepted may be particularly prone to trying self-injury if others around them are doing so. There is concern that contemporary media may be inadvertently fostering the spread of self-injury and making it normalized, or appear more acceptable or common than it actually is, and this could explain why young people are increasingly engaging in self-injury.

The Link to Attachment

Attachment has a direct impact on a person's ability to develop an effective emotional response system—something that is compromised for many who self-injure. Attachment develops when a child is repeatedly comforted and cared for, and his or her needs are consistently met. Attachment to a caregiver provides a safe space to learn to control emotions and to develop healthy relationships and a positive self-image.

Successful attachment allows children to develop a core of resiliency and a sense that they can call upon their own strengths when facing difficult situations. However, problems with attachment during the first few years of life can cause children to have trouble controlling, expressing, or understanding emotions as they grow, which is a risk factor for self-injury.

Exposure to Trauma

There is a growing body of evidence that trauma and stress can impact brain development, increasing the body's physiological reaction to stress while decreasing the brain's ability to respond to stress in a thoughtful way. Approximately half of those who self-injure have experienced or witnessed trauma and/or loss. Although the scientific study of trauma is still young, there are some emerging explanations for why those who have experienced trauma may self-injure. There is also increasing evidence that severe trauma may alter both the structure and the chemistry of the brain and other body systems involved in stress.

Normally, after a stressful event like a car crash, individuals will relive their memories, emotions, and sensations. This mental replaying and processing of the event helps defuse the emotional content and allows people to put the event behind them and move on. However, highly traumatic events—such as child abuse, being caught in a disaster, a severe car crash, or experiencing sexual assault involving both heightened emotions and dissociation—can cause memories to fragment. Unlike normal memories with a complete narrative, these traumatic memories are reexperienced as vivid sensations with all their original emotional intensity. The trauma is not processed into something of the past but is perceived by the body as an ongoing threat. Remaining at a heightened sense of alertness over time, survivors of trauma lose the ability to control and monitor their response to stress. Eventually, any and all feelings seem enormously threatening.

Being unable to control one's own emotions can deeply damage an individual's sense of self. These people are left feeling different, defec-

Self-injury sometimes develops out of a need to get other people to listen or take notice of emotional distress. For some individuals, this begins with dramatic changes in clothing, hair, and behavior.

Social Media and Self-Injury

There is ongoing debate about the value of the many Internet sites that contain content on self-injury. Professional therapists are concerned about sites that portray self-injury as a normal coping strategy for dealing with life's challenges and struggles. Many of these leave out discussion or descriptions of the consequences of self-injury—the trips to the doctor to treat injuries that are more severe than intended; the feelings of shame and disgust after self-injuring; and the scars, lies, and fear of being discovered. Some therapists worry about social contagion—the spread of self-injury through the adoption and even glorification of behaviors seen online.

Others point to social media as a place where those who self-injure can express themselves, find acceptance, and be understood. The Internet is a place where people who self-injure can build relationships that are important for recovery and be part of a community that supports their efforts to deal with powerful emotions and difficult situations. It can also serve as a place where they can help others. The trick seems to be to realize that online relationships, although important, are not a substitute for in-person relationships or the work of recovery with a trusted and skilled therapist. It is also critical to know who is behind the information posted and what their goals are, as well as to look for biased content.

tive, out of control, and unable to comfort themselves or allow others to do so. They may enter abusive relationships, engage in risk-taking behaviors, and/or self-injure in an attempt to understand and process the original trauma and integrate their fragmented memories. In essence the person is trying to take control of his or her emotions. This action says, "I'm in control of who hurts me. I hurt myself."

Links to Other Mental Health Conditions

Self-injury often coexists with or is a symptom of another mental health issue. In fact, self-injury was long thought to be a symptom of other disorders, and early studies of self-injury looked only at people hospitalized for mental health issues or receiving clinical treatment.

Borderline personality disorder is closely tied to self-injury: About 70 percent to 75 percent of those with this disorder self-injure. Self-injury is also associated with depression—approximately 42 percent of those with depression self-injure. People who suffer from anxiety disorders—the most common emotional disorder in the United States—may also turn to self-injury as a way to feel calm and find relief from their symptoms. Self-injury and eating disorders often co-occur, especially among females. A 2011 study reported in the *Journal of Adolescent Health* of almost fifteen hundred adolescents with eating disorders found that among those screened for self-injury, more than 40 percent self-injured. Finally, PTSD also has links to self-injury. A 2007 study of US military veterans diagnosed with PTSD found that 54 percent had self-injured within the two weeks prior to participating in the study.

Although it is now recognized that those without other mental health issues self-injure, those with mental health issues self-injure at a higher rate. It is estimated that 40 percent to 60 percent of teens living with other mental health issues and 19 percent to 25 percent of adults living with mental health issues self-injure. That is three to four times the number of people who self-injure but who have not been diagnosed with other mental health issues.

For many, self-injury begins as a way of coping with other mental health conditions and can be a symptom of the underlying mental health issue. However, for some, self-injury can become the primary way of coping and take on a life of its own. "I realized I didn't have to feel, I didn't have to suffer, because I could cut,"[34] says a young woman remembering her experience with self-injury over many years.

Other Risk Factors

Other risk factors have emerged as researchers and therapists struggle to understand the underlying causes of self-injury. Chemical imbalances in the brain or physiological differences are believed to be a contributing factor. These can include low serotonin levels, imbalances of the opioid and dopamine systems, stronger-than-usual physiological responses to stress, and/or less tolerance of stress.

Some people who self-injure have what is called a negative cognitive style. This is the tendency to believe that negative life events are due to stable causes that will persist over time, rather than a temporary condition. They tend to believe that things are their fault rather than something having to do with the world around them. People with negative cognitive styles tend to believe that something bad will not change, that it will affect many aspects of their life, and that it is their fault. It is very difficult for them to see negative life events as temporary situations that will get better over time. All of this can contribute to the hopelessness that puts people at risk for self-injury.

Self-injury also appears to be linked to impulsivity—the tendency to respond to feelings or desires quickly without being able to wait and think things through. In fact, self-injury is often an impulsive act. Steven Jellá, cofounder of Rooted Transformation Therapeutic Services and associate executive director at San Diego Youth Services, reports that most people self-injure for the first time on impulse—they are feeling bad and see something they can use to hurt themselves. Studies have shown that almost half of teens who self-injure have thought about the act less than an hour prior to injuring themselves, with many self-injuring within a few minutes of getting the urge.

A Variety of Reasons

Studies have shown that people self-injure for a variety of functional reasons but that difficulty handling and communicating strong emotions, being exposed to trauma, suffering from co-occurring mental health issues, and dissociation all put people at heightened risk for self-injury. In addition, researchers have found hopelessness is a key difference between those who self-injure and those who do not. Those who have parental support and/or feel they have personal potential are less likely to self-injure.

CHAPTER 3

What Is It like to Live with Self-Injury?

Living with self-injury can feel like being caught in a continuous cycle. For some, every strong feeling is a new and uncomfortable experience that is difficult to process. For others, there is a buildup of emotions or an emptiness that becomes intolerable. Or something may happen that puts a person over the edge—breaking up with a boyfriend, failing a test, stress over an upcoming athletic competition, a snide remark that hurts. It is rarely the same thing each time that overwhelms the person. What is consistent, however, is the need to find a way to release the tension and make the feeling of deadness, anxiety, anger, fear, or badness go away.

The Cycle of Cutting

The release that comes with self-injury is only temporary, so that when emotions build again, or feelings of emptiness threaten to overwhelm, it is easy to turn to self-injury once more for relief, and the cycle continues. Journalist Marilee Strong, who spent years interviewing people who self-injure, noted in her book *A Bright Red Scream: Self-Mutilation and the Language of Pain*:

> The scores of "cutters" I interviewed for this book and the hundreds I have spoken to in the ensuing decade told me that carving and scratching their skin with knives made them feel *better*. Purposeful, repetitive, controlled self-injury released and relieved them from overwhelming feelings of tension and anxiety. It grounded and reintegrated them, and enabled them to break out of numbing states of dissociation in which

People who self-injure are seeking relief. Some cut or scrape their skin; others burn themselves, punch a wall, or pick a fight—anything to relieve the tension or emptiness inside .

they had felt they were slipping into nothingness. The pain they were inflicting on their bodies was nothing compared to the intolerable emotional pain they felt inside. The blood that flowed and the wounds that formed made them feel alive, whole, real, human.[35]

Self-injurers often feel overwhelmed and need to get back to a place where it is possible to deal with life again. Sometimes the self-injury is impulsive and the urge too strong to resist. A knife or sharp object close at hand is used to cut or scrape, or a pin is stuck into one's arm over and over again; other times it may mean burning oneself, punching a wall, or picking a fight with someone bigger who is sure to do damage.

Other times there is an emotional buildup; the knowledge that punishment is needed or a slow accumulation of feelings that become more and more intolerable. Vanessa Vega writes of this feeling in her book, *Comes the Darkness, Comes the Light*:

> The darkness started coming for me on Monday . . . the slight but undeniable tingling that just won't go away. . . . I throw myself into a flurry of activity; if I run hard and fast enough, maybe I can beat it this time. Sometimes that works. But not this time. . . . By Wednesday, the darkness is in my dreams. I am hurt. I am alone. I am dead. By Thursday, I start to shake. I know what is going to happen and I feel powerless to fight it. I read a book. Flip through a magazine. Flip channels on the television. Anything to take my mind off what I know is to come. . . . By Friday morning I have shut down. I am so far into myself that if I were to withdraw any more, I would implode. . . . I'm so tired. I don't want to do this. I desperately try to think of errands I have to do before I go home . . . but not today. Today, there is only the darkness and it waits for me.[36]

While some injure impulsively, others make what can be elaborate preparations. They make arrangements to self-injure, and lay out the tools they plan to use. "People with this disorder may brood about harming themselves for hours and even days and may go through a ritualistic sequence of behaviors, such as tracing areas of their skin, and compulsively putting their self-harm paraphernalia in order,"[37] says psychiatrist Armando R. Favazza. For example, Vega had a very specific ritual for her cutting. She would lay out her cotton balls, alcohol, and scissors and make sure everything was perfectly

"People with this disorder may brood about harming themselves for hours and even days and may go through a ritualistic sequence of behaviors, such as tracing areas of their skin, and compulsively putting their self-harm paraphernalia in order."[37]

—Psychiatrist Armando R. Favazza.

clean. Her ritual was so precise that if anything interfered, if she messed up, or if she did not cut enough, the self-injury would not "count" and she would have to start all over again.

When injuring themselves, many people report feeling no pain. They appear to dissociate or enter a trance-like state in which they are oblivious to what they are doing. They are not really aware of their actions, although the extent of the injury is usually carefully controlled and carried out. Some studies suggest that those with a history of self-injury have a higher threshold for pain or a conditioned response to stress that produces higher levels of endorphins that block the sensation of pain. British researchers have shown the presence of higher levels of endorphins among people who self-injure and found that the levels drop off when people stop self-injuring. Vega talks about time standing still. "I don't know how long I've been cutting. Part of me can see my arm, but there isn't any pain, and so I don't know if it's real."[38] At some point she always stopped, but she talks about not knowing when or why she did.

> "If I don't bleed, I don't feel better. The sight of my own blood spilling forth sets me back in control. I like to think when I cut, 'Okay, now all the pain in your head is in your skin.'"[40]
>
> —A sixteen-year-old female.

Other people need to feel the pain of the injury. The pain, the sight of blood, and the endorphins produced by the body all change the way the person feels and provide relief from the emotions or lack of emotions that had threatened to swamp the person prior to the self-injury. A twenty-year-old female describes her experience with self-injury as using "very bitter medicine" and states, "If I liked the pain, then it wouldn't help. I hate it. That's why it helps. . . . The blood means I hurt enough to chase away all other pain."[39] As one sixteen-year-old put it, "If I don't bleed, I don't feel better. The sight of my own blood spilling forth sets me back in control. I like to think when I cut, 'Okay, now all the pain in your head is in your skin.'"[40]

After the emotions driving the self-injury are gone, the individual needs to focus on the injury. Often basic first aid is needed. The wound needs to be cleaned and bandaged. The tools need to be hidden away.

Signs and Symptoms of Self-Injury

The signs and symptoms of self-injury can include any number of the following:

- Scars from cuts or burns

- Fresh cuts, scratches, bruises or other wounds

- Wounds that never seem to heal

- Broken bones

- Keeping sharp objects on hand

- Wearing long sleeves and/or long pants, even in hot weather

- Frequent "accidents"

- Spending a lot of time alone

- Continual difficulties with relationships

- Mood swings and impulsive behavior

For some this is a practical part of taking care of themselves. For others the wound gives them permission to pamper themselves, to take the time to take care of themselves even if they typically feel they are not worthy of special treatment. It is also a time to decide what to say should anyone notice and ask about the injury. Most people who self-injure will have thought of an excuse—perhaps that they tripped or bumped into something or were careless and accidently cut themselves.

The Fear of Discovery

Because the idea of hurting oneself on purpose is not commonly accepted and appalls many people, those who self-injure will usually hurt a part of the body that can be hidden. Arms and legs can be covered with long sleeves or long pants. The stomach, chest, or more private areas, such as the breasts, are also typically covered by clothes and hidden from others. Unless the person who self-injures is one of the rare people who self-injure in the company or presence of others, self-injurers usually do not tell anyone what they have done. "Do the right thing," Vega says she used to say to herself. "Keep this sorrow to yourself. If you share it, you're only going to bring other people down."[41]

Part of this is the fear of how others will react. Part of it may be the person's own feelings of shame or disgust or worry about what they are doing to themselves and the fear that someone will discover it. "Afterwards, after I bandaged and cleaned myself up, the shame set in," reports one woman. "I hated myself for having done something so strange. I hated myself for not being able to deal with my feelings. I hated myself for not having control and being afraid and risking someone finding out."[42] In the words of another young woman who used to self-injure, "It makes you feel better immediately, but in the long run, it makes you feel worse. When you cut, you generally end up feeling ashamed that you hurt yourself and embarrassed by the scratches and self-injury scars."[43]

The physical scars of cutting can be vivid and long-lasting. For this reason, individuals who self-injure typically inflict harm to parts of the body that can be covered with clothing.

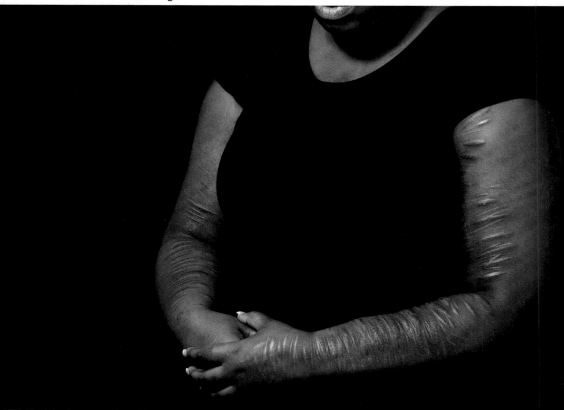

The shame and fear of discovery can cause someone who self-injures to withdraw and become isolated from others, leaving them with fewer people to talk to and fewer options for dealing with their emotions. Therefore, when the feelings come back the cycle begins again. "When the blade cut the surface and I saw blood, it would bring everything back into focus," says one twenty-five-year-old who self-injures. "But it didn't work for very long so I'd have to do it over and over."[44]

As Steven Levenkron, a psychotherapist who has worked with those who self-injure, notes in his book *Cutting: Understanding and Overcoming Self-Mutilation*, "Cutting never really puts the feelings of being hurt to rest, but rather provides only short-term relief. Thus taking this route leads not only to a build up of bad feelings, but also to an addiction to the method itself for the relief it provides."[45]

> "When the blade cut the surface and I saw blood, it would bring everything back into focus. But it didn't work for very long so I'd have to do it over and over."[44]
>
> —A twenty-five-year-old female.

Differences in How Males and Females Self-Injure

Some studies have found that there is a difference in the way males and females self-injure. It has been proposed that females, in general, have been taught to internalize anger, pain, and aggression and are thus more likely to take their troubles out on themselves than others. A 2011 study reported in the *Journal of American College Health*, found that females were more likely to use self-injury to deal with their emotions, as a form of self-control, or because they experienced an overwhelming urge. In addition, almost all females who self-injure do so in private.

In contrast, researchers suggest that it is more socially acceptable for males to show aggression. Studies find male-preferred forms of self-injury, such as punching and hitting things, can look like outward aggression, even if the real intent is to harm themselves. Some males will pick fights, injure others, or put themselves in harm's way with the intent of injuring themselves. They are more likely to report anger as the emotion behind self-injury than females, and some look to self-injury as a way to get a rush or surge of energy. Males are more likely to have been drunk or high the first time they self-injured and to self-injure in front of others. Males may also first experience self-injury in a group setting via a "courage" game that tests members' ability to tolerate pain.

Dealing with the Injury and the Aftermath

Even minor injuries require care and time to heal. People typically hide their injuries so others will not notice them. Some of those who self-injure will prolong the pain of their self-injury by ripping off the bandage to disrupt the scab or pick at the wound to keep it from healing. For some, keeping a wound active can delay the need to injure themselves again.

Sometimes, an injury does not heal. Infection can set in and require a trip to the doctor or even to the emergency room. Or an injury may be more severe than intended. A knife may go too deep and damage blood vessels, tendons, muscles, or nerves and require immediate medical attention, hospitalization, even surgery to repair. One male college student, a cross-country runner, cut the arch of his foot so badly that he severed tendons and needed orthopedic surgery in order to regain use of his toes so he could walk properly again. Bones can break in ways that are difficult to reset. Head banging can cause concussions. A severed tendon may be difficult to repair. In these cases even the best medical treatment may not be able to put things right. The individual may need physical therapy, surgery, or ongoing medical treatment and may have to deal with permanent disabilities: a hand that will not work properly, a permanent limp, the loss of sensation in several fingers.

A quick swipe of a knife led one young woman to almost lose her life to self-injury. After cutting herself more deeply than intended, she required two units of blood, treatment for shock, and microsurgery to repair the veins, tendons, and nerves in her wrist. She was left with a long road to recovery. Speaking of the injury, she said, "It will

Self-Injury and Eating Disorders

The fact that self-injury and eating disorders often co-occur makes sense. The two behaviors share many of the same underlying causes and serve many of the same functions.

Both self-injury and eating disorders are frequently driven by trauma, especially sexual abuse, and can serve as a way to gain control over the body after control was ripped away. They are way of saying, "I'm in control of who hurts me. I control my own pain." Self-injury, anorexia, and bulimia can all be used to feel relief from overwhelming feelings of tension, anger, emptiness, and self-hatred and as a way to punish oneself for something that is mistakenly believed to be one's fault. Both bulimia and self-injury tend to be impulsive, secretive, and ritualistic and often involve shame and guilt.

Psychiatrist Armando R. Favazza, an expert on self-injury, regards self-injury and eating disorders as part of a cluster of interchangeable impulsive behaviors that includes periodic alcohol and drug abuse and makes up what he calls repetitive self-mutilation syndrome. "Patients may start out with one of these symptoms and go on to develop any of the others."

Quoted in Marilee Strong, *A Bright Red Scream: Self-Mutilation and the Language of Pain.* New York: Penguin, 2009, p. 117.

be a year before they even know if my hand will ever work again. The stuff I did to protect me from my life may make me a cripple for life."[46] In this way scars and damage from self-injury become a permanent part of living.

Janis Whitlock and her colleagues found that "just over one in five (21.2%) of [those who self-injured] indicated that they had injured themselves more severely than expected." In addition, "over one-third (39.6%) felt they should have sought medical care but did not."[47] For those who seek care, most medical personnel are not used to treating patients with self-inflicted wounds who are likely to create new injuries soon after they are treated. "The self-inflicted nature of [self-injury] is challenging and sometimes infuriating to many health care professionals," writes Strong. "Self-injurers are seen widely as a problematic and hopeless group within the health care system—especially in situations where resources are scarce, time available from doctors and nurses is measured in precious minutes, and compassion is stretched to the limit."[48]

Seeking medical treatment can also raise questions about suicide. Some injuries may be mistaken for a suicide attempt. The person may be hospitalized for inpatient psychiatric treatment, and the tools the person used to self-injure may be taken away.

Self-Injury as an Addiction

Over time some people who originally self-injured to cope with an immediate need can begin to rely on self-injury to manage their emotions. By pairing self-injury with the relief it provides, self-injury becomes the solution, the thing to turn to for relief when emotions get too intense. These individuals begin to define themselves as "cutters," and the fact they self-injure becomes part of their identity.

People who have self-injured over long periods claim that compared to alcohol or drug addictions and even eating disorders, self-injury is harder to give up. In the words of one young woman, "It really is like an addiction. You do it the first time and see how much better you feel. Then when you feel bad again you think, 'Hey that cutting thing helped.' So you start doing it every time you feel bad."[49]

In this way self-injury becomes a constant feature of life. People may become so sensitive to emotions that the mere anticipation of emotion produces the urge to self-injure. Self-injury may become an impulse, used without thought as quickly and unconsciously as someone might bite his or her nails. As people increasingly define themselves as "cutters," they may come to believe that self-injury is an integral part of their lives. They may believe that if they are prevented from self-injuring, they will fall apart completely. In the words of one woman who has been cutting on and off for thirty years, "I always felt I'd die if I *didn't* cut."[50]

The body's release of endorphins when injured may contribute to an addiction-withdrawal cycle, in which individuals only feel com-

The amount of damage inflicted during self-injury varies greatly depending on the individual and the method used. One study found that 21 percent of young people who self-injured hurt themselves more severely than expected. Of this group, 35.3 percent were injured severely enough that they should have seen a doctor; however, only 6.5 percent actually sought medical attention.

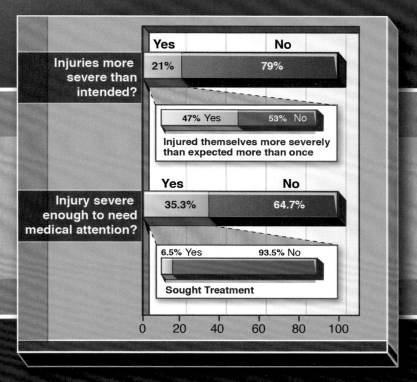

Source: J.L. Whitlock and M. Selekman, "Non-Suicidal Self-Injury (NSSI) Across the Lifespan," in M. Nock, ed., *Oxford Handbook of Suicide and Self-Injury.* Oxford, England: Oxford University Press, 2014. www.selfinjury.bctr.cornell.edu.

fortable when their endorphin levels are high. Like a true addiction, self-injury can be progressive and grow more frequent and more severe over time. This is why some experts have grouped self-injury together with eating disorders, sexual compulsions, and other pain-driven syndromes. Psychotherapist Dusty Miller writes, "I am now convinced that all self-harm must be understood and treated like an addiction."[51]

Living with Underlying Mental Health Issues

Many people who self-injure also suffer from other mental health issues, including borderline personality disorder, depression, post-traumatic stress, anxiety, and eating disorders. They struggle to cope with attachment disorders or must deal with the trauma or abuse they have experienced. Their daily lives therefore involve coping not just with the cycle of and fallout from self-injury, but also the impacts of these other disorders.

Of particular difficulty for those who self-injure are maintaining relationships with others and dealing with their own emotions. Those with borderline personality disorder can be afraid of being alone and must cope with dramatic mood swings. They may also behave impulsively, have trouble controlling their anger, and blame others for things that go wrong. All of these make it difficult to hold down a job, attend school, and maintain relationships. Similarly, those with anxiety or PTSD may suffer nightmares and painful memories, and they may have to cope with feelings of panic and/or fear that can strike without warning or linger just under the surface. Those with depression may struggle with a lack of energy and interest in the world, have poor concentration, have difficulty making decisions, and have trouble remembering details. They may feel sad, anxious, and empty and must cope with feelings of worthlessness, guilt, and hopelessness.

Finally, alcohol abuse, drug abuse, and/or eating disorders are other problems that people who self-injure may have to cope with. Those who use alcohol or drugs to mask or dull pain are left in an altered state with impaired judgment and less control over their behavior. People who self-injure while under the influence of alcohol or drugs are at the highest risk for inflicting serious injuries that go beyond what was intended, leading to months of recovery, permanent disabilities, or unintentional death.

CHAPTER 4

Can Self-Injury Be Treated or Cured?

It is possible to recover from self-injury, although the journey is different for each person. For some the need to self-injure may disappear as the crisis or situation that was overwhelming the individual resolves. But for many the road to recovery can be long and challenging.

The heart of successful treatment for self-injury seems to be understanding the role self-injury plays for each unique individual and addressing the feelings and situations that lead to the compulsion to self-injure. If these are not resolved, the person will likely fall back on self-injury or replace self-injury with another destructive behavior such as alcohol or drug abuse, an eating disorder, or sex and relationship addictions. "[Treatment] is an incremental process of slowly letting go of the self-injurious behavior while adding more acceptable behaviors and communication skills. Structure, safety, and consistency are central,"[52] say psychotherapists Judy A. Stone and Shari M. Sias.

Experts note that in general, the longer someone has self-injured, the greater the challenge to stop. Thus, the sooner a person seeks and/or receives treatment, the better. Treatments that have the greatest chance of success include a combination of medication and psychotherapy, and a focus on learning to handle emotions and adopting new, healthier coping strategies. A female college student summed up her experience: "Recovery from self-injury is about giving up a way of life that's attached to emotional pain and suffering, and when I let this happen, the self-injury is not an issue because I don't need it."[53]

Many people want to stop self-injuring but do not know how else to cope with the feelings that overwhelm them. They may lack the language to describe the feelings in words and may not feel comfortable asking for help. People who have been abused may not believe they can trust anyone and may feel forced to deal with their problems on their own. Or they may think they are so flawed no one can help or would want to waste their time doing so. Those who have self-injured for a long time may fear giving up their main coping mechanism. Says one fifty-three-year-old woman, "It would be nice to put [self-injury] aside, but that would be like asking someone who smoked a pack a day for thirty years to imagine doing without cigarettes."[54] Despite these difficulties, finding someone to trust and confiding in him or her is a huge but important step in the recovery from self-injury.

> "Recovery from self-injury is about giving up a way of life that's attached to emotional pain and suffering, and when I let this happen, the self-injury is not an issue because I don't need it."[53]
>
> —A female college student.

The Search for Treatment

Self-injury can inspire various negative reactions, including shock, disgust, withdrawal, negative statements and judgments, anxiety, fear, anger, and confusion. Patrick L. Kerr of the West Virginia University School of Medicine and his colleagues note, "Strong reactions to someone's disclosure of self-injury are common and understandable. This is true among the general public, medical professionals in all disciplines, and some behavioral health care providers despite their extensive training in the treatment of behavioral disorders."[55]

As a result, those seeking help with self-injury often bounce from therapist to therapist and have unsatisfying or negative experiences that turn them away from treatment. Says Barent Walsh, executive director of The Bridge in central Massachusetts, "It's not unusual that self-injurers encounter professionals who respond clumsily to their self-harm behaviors."[56] This bears out in research. For example, "conversations with others about their [self-injury] were rated as being mostly *un*helpful"[57] by the college students Jennifer Muehlen-kamp and her colleagues surveyed.

Often therapists react strongly to patients' injuries and try to get them to "contract for safety," which means to sign an agreement that they will stop self-injuring. However, some view this as unsupportive and largely for the therapist's comfort. According to Walsh, "Asking individuals to give up self-injury when it is their best emotion-regulation technique can be both unrealistic and invalidating. Clients may view efforts to contract for safety as an implicit form of condemnation. A more effective strategy is to emphasize that the client learn new skills to regulate emotions."[58]

Strong negative reactions to self-injury are a barrier to therapy. The individual seeking help is likely not to return or may decide that

Gaining an understanding of the feelings and situations that lead to self-injury is essential for recovery. Those who do not resolve these issues will fall back on self-injury or might end up searching for relief in drug use or other unhealthy practices.

How to Help Someone Who Self-Injures

Experts say it is important to be nonjudgmental when trying to help people who self-injure. In other words, try not to criticize or judge their injuries or react with horror or disgust. Instead, help the individual care for his or her injuries and let the person know they are important and loved. Sometimes sharing personal coping strategies can give those who self-injure ideas for other ways to cope. Helping those who self-injure expand their social networks and develop relationships with others can also help them feel they are worthy of another's attention and/or have others to talk with and perhaps express their feelings and emotions.

For friends and family of those who self-injure, learning more about self-injury can help. Staying in close contact with the therapist who is treating their loved one can also provide additional information on what can be done to support him or her. Family and friends need to find a way to take care of themselves so that they can be strong enough to help someone else. This might include joining a support group and/or doing things that keep them healthy, renew their energy, and help them cope with difficult situations that involve their loved one.

the therapist cannot handle or be trusted with the truth. As one twenty-two-year-old male put it, "Don't tell me I'm sick, don't tell me to stop. Don't try to make me feel guilty, that's how I feel already. Listen to me, support me, help me."[59]

On the other hand, experts warn that strong expressions in support of self-injury are also problematic, since they can encourage more self-injury. What most experts typically advise is a respectful curiosity, so that there can be a conversation and exploration of what self-injury does for the person who is seeking help. For example, the simple question "What does cutting do for you?" brought the following response from a patient: "At last someone will actually talk to me about this and not treat me like I'm a psycho and want me to stop immediately."[60] This powerful statement from a young woman underscores the need for conversation and exploration as the underpinning of therapy.

Mark Schwartz, a psychologist based in St. Louis who ran a successful treatment program for people who self-injure, thinks most mental health professionals have not done a good job of listening to their patients. "What they try to do is to medicate the syndrome, call it a disease, cure it, get it under control, twelve-step it—anything but respect the symptom and realize there's a damn good reason that the person feels and acts this way." Schwartz believes chronic self-injury is a way for the person to try to relive, understand, and deal with past trauma. With that in mind, he says, "if you simply use the symptom as a window, you'll eventually find out what happened to the person and be able to relieve them of that symptom. As soon as the brain is able to talk about and process the traumatic event, the person is no longer doomed to replay it."[61]

Since approximately half of those who self-injure have experienced trauma and/or loss, a trauma-based approach to therapy makes sense and can allow people to reclaim their lives so they are no longer haunted by their past. Trauma-based therapy helps people learn to attach words to terror and integrate their fragmented memories so that the trauma no longer needs to be replayed over and over in an attempt to understand it. "There is something about surviving the memory of trauma, telling someone, getting it out. It doesn't erase the memory but it puts it in perspective," says Scott Lines, a psychologist in San Francisco. "I think that's why with treatment the behavior changes."[62] Research is increasingly discovering the brain's ability to be flexible and adapt. Those who have experienced trauma do not necessarily need to remain in its grip.

> "At last someone will actually talk to me about this and not treat me like I'm a psycho and want me to stop immediately."[60]
>
> —A twenty-year-old female college student.

Key Components of Therapy for Self-Injury

Understanding what self-injury does for the individual is the start of meaningful treatment. For example, if self-injury is mostly used to deal with overwhelming emotions, than treatment will need to focus on reducing emotional triggers, helping the individual learn to tolerate emotional discomfort, and teaching other ways to cope. On the other hand, if the person primarily uses self-injury to communicate with or control others, then communication and social skills trainings need to be the focus of treatment.

According to Walsh, "Understanding self-injury requires clinicians to consider both the intrapersonal and interpersonal functions."[63] In other words, treatment must include recognizing what self-injury does for the person in terms of his or her relationships with others. Internal functions might include creating a feeling of peace and calm, stopping the mind from racing, relieving anger or self-hate, or punishing oneself. Interpersonal functions can include the desire to communicate, coerce others, compete with other self-injurers, resolve conflicts, or generate intimacy.

There are a number of other factors a therapist will likely want to explore to better understand the role self-injury plays, including what triggers it, what happens afterward, how it makes the person feel, how the person cares for his or her injuries, and if the person has any routines associated with the behavior. The goal is to develop alternate behaviors that can fulfill the same functions but are less risky and cause less bodily harm.

Experts also suggest that examining the wounds (if modesty permits) can help the therapist see both the extent of the injuries and how recent they are. This gives the therapist objective data with which to work. In addition, by showing his or her injuries, the act of self-injury is no longer hidden, which is a change for most people who self-injure. New York psychotherapist Steven Levenkron explains the power of this act in the following way:

> This revealing of a once-secret defense devalues it. It should be done at the beginning of each session until the cutting stops. If the cutter is aware that the cut will be examined after each episode, she will begin to imagine that the therapist is attending the episode at the time of its occurrence and analyzing the reason for doing it. Eventually the anticipated analysis of the reason for it replaces the act of cutting.[64]

In general, altering habits or rituals associated with self-injury can make it easier for patients to change future behavior. Stone and Sias summarized this approach in describing the goals for one woman's treatment plan: "The point was not for her to rid herself of anything but to accept uncomfortable feelings like anger and sadness as just uncomfortable not 'terrible.'"[65]

Types of Therapy Available for Self-Injury

There are a number of different types of psychotherapy used to treat those who self-injure. But in order for people who self-injure to accept help, they must believe they are worthy of it. They must also trust that the therapist will not betray them or turn on them if they reveal the horror of who they believe themselves to be. Nienke Kool and her colleagues, who interviewed people who had self-injured for years, report that every survivor with whom they spoke said, "Learning to cope with their inner selves and others was an important skill to reduce and stop self-injury."[66]

The traditional first line for therapy is psychodynamic psychotherapy. This therapy is based on the idea that a person's behavior is affected by the unconscious mind and by past experiences. It involves exploring the entire range of a patient's emotions, including contradictory feelings, feelings that are troubling or threatening, and feelings that the patient may not have recognized or acknowledged in the past. As the therapy progresses, the resulting patterns of behavior and feelings become apparent. The focus is then to make the patient aware of how past experience and the unconscious mind are affecting his or her present life. The goal is to foster the internal resources needed to deal with and effectively manage the problem.

Another therapy, and one that some studies show works particularly well for those who self-injure, is cognitive behavioral therapy (CBT). CBT focuses on examining the relationships between thoughts, feelings, and behaviors and exploring patterns of thinking that lead to self-destructive actions. CBT is different from traditional psychodynamic psychotherapy in that the therapist and the patient actively work together to help the patient modify his or her patterns of thinking to improve coping skills. Studies have shown that CBT

Assistance from a qualified therapist can help self-injurers regain control over their lives. This is especially important for those who have experienced traumatic events.

actually improves brain activity in people with mental illness, which suggests that the brain is changing the way it functions as a result of the therapy.

Another type of therapy that seems to work well for those who self-injure is dialectical behavior therapy (DBT). DBT is a modification of CBT that was specifically developed to treat chronically suicidal and self-injurious individuals with borderline personality disorder. DBT differs from traditional CBT in that it emphasizes validation—the acceptance of uncomfortable thoughts, feelings, and behavior—and uses mindfulness practice and other relaxation techniques. Mindfulness is a modern reworking of ancient meditation traditions, principally from Buddhist traditions. It is based on the idea that strong emotions can overwhelm and incapacitate a person. Unhelpful thoughts may accompany these emotions, such as "I'll never get over this" or "I must be stupid." Such thoughts are often accepted without thinking and tend to perpetuate strong emotions, so that the individual loses control of conscious thought and becomes unable to cope.

The aim of mindfulness therapy is to help the individual be aware of his or her thoughts and bodily sensations and to create a different, easier relationship with problematic thoughts. Through this practice, an individual develops the ability to accept distressing thoughts without self-criticism and to tolerate self-destructive urges (such as the desire to cut oneself) without acting on them.

Types of Medication for Self-Injury

Although more research has been done on therapeutic approaches for self-injury, there is evidence that medication may also help reduce the frequency of self-injury. Medication can work to address immediate symptoms and help individuals tolerate exploring the issues that underlie their problem. Four different types of medication have been used to treat self-injury: antidepressants, opioid antagonists, mood stabilizers, and antipsychotics.

Antidepressants such as Prozac and Zoloft impact the neurotransmitter serotonin and are frequently used to treat depression, borderline personality disorder, and the impulsiveness and/or aggression often associated with self-injury. They act to slow the breakdown of serotonin in the brain so that the level of serotonin remains higher longer (low serotonin levels are associated with impulsivity and depression). Antidepressants can sometimes be very successful in decreasing the number and frequency of self-injuries, particularly in those with compulsive self-injuries like hair pulling and picking at real or imaginary wounds. They also seem to reduce the need to immediately act on a desire to self-injure, helping the person wait for the sensation to pass.

Opioid antagonists such as Naltrexone block release of the body's natural opioids (endorphins) and take away the euphoric high or the sensation of well-being that some who self-injure crave. These medications help individuals who may have become used to high levels of endorphins in childhood as a result of repeated exposure to physical or sexual abuse. As adults, these individuals may need above-normal levels of endorphins to cope with stress and/or have trouble with their opioid system, which may be a contributing factor to their self-injury. The idea is that if nothing is gained by self-injury, people will stop the behavior.

Mood stabilizers such as Tegretol (brand name) or its generic, carbamazepine, have been shown to help treat mental health issues linked to self-injury, such as depression, anxiety, mood swings, and racing thoughts. Mood stabilizers act on neurotransmitters to help control emotions, behaviors, and seizures. They have been found to decrease impulsive aggression and help people gain control over behaviors such as overdoses, self-injury, violence, and rage.

Antipsychotics such as Zyprexa or Clozaril (generic name clozapine) have been used to treat impulsive aggression, especially among those with borderline personality disorder, which often occurs in association with self-injury. Antipsychotic drugs help regulate the functioning of brain circuits that control thinking, mood, and perception.

Medication can help, but as Rex Cowdry of the National Institute of Mental Health says, "Don't expect a magic bullet. Almost invariably, [medications] need to be used in conjunction with psychotherapy, because self-injury is often a long-established pattern tied up with significant difficulties in relationships and other behaviors that have developed."[67] In addition, some medication can cause people to feel removed from their feelings and life around them. This may contribute to more self-injury if these individuals self-injure because they feel disconnected from the world around them. Medications need to be prescribed with careful consideration of each patient's unique circumstances.

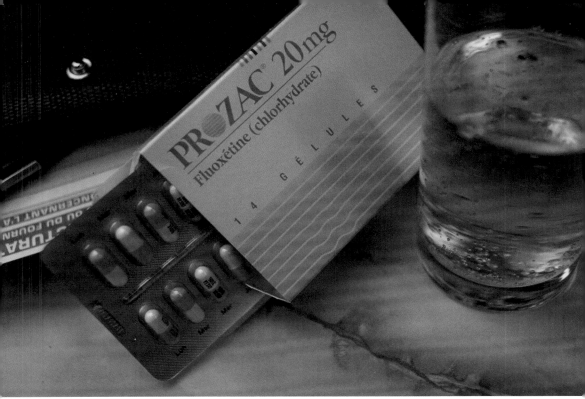

Antidepressants such as Prozac are frequently prescribed for treatment of conditions that are associated with self-injury: depression, impulsiveness, and aggression. These types of drugs have shown success in decreasing the number and frequency of self-injuries.

Hospitalization for Psychiatric Treatment

Those who self-injure may be hospitalized to receive more intensive therapy and/or treat other associated mental health conditions such as depression, a suicide attempt, an eating disorder, or another underlying mental health issue. Hospitalization can be used to treat self-injury by providing a safe environment and access to frequent and intense psychotherapy. The closed and regulated environment blocks access to tools that can be used for self-injury and also removes the person from the pressures of daily life. This can create the space needed to focus on treatment and recovery.

During hospitalization, peers can provide support and help keep other patients honest about their feelings and actions. Intensive therapy at time when the person is feeling out of control can provide the space to learn that thoughts, feelings, and actions are all separate and not a chain of events that must always lead to the same conclusion.

Eye Movement Desensitization and Reprocessing

Eye movement desensitization and reprocessing (EMDR) is a new technique that helps release the impact of traumatic memories. It involves a patient remembering a traumatic event while watching a therapist's finger as the therapist moves the finger rapidly back and forth before the patient's eyes. This is repeated until the person no longer feels panic and anxiety with the memory of the trauma. Then the process is repeated while the patient thinks positive thoughts, again while following the therapist's finger back and forth.

Although the technique sounds strange to those unfamiliar with it, several studies have shown that EMDR can significantly reduce anxiety during the first session. How it works, not even its inventor, psychologist Francine Shapiro of Palo Alto, California, knows. The theory is that EMDR stimulates the brain to process and metabolize fragmented memories without having to recall and verbalize each of the person's traumatic memories. EMDR has been successful at reducing the frequency and intensity of intrusive thoughts, flashbacks, and nightmares as well as ongoing anxiety. Since these can all contribute to self-injury, EMDR can help address the underlying problems that may cause a person to self-injure.

In other words, anger does not have to result in violence, and uncomfortable thoughts need not lead to self-injury. Such treatment can offer an opportunity to create new, positive self-messages and try out new coping strategies.

Help for Those Who Self-Injure

Those who self-injure can best help themselves by seeking assistance. This means telling someone they are self-injuring, seeking help to understand why they do it, and finding other ways of coping. Part of this includes learning to recognize situations or feelings that trigger the desire to self-injure, connecting with others who will support them so that they do not feel alone, and learning to express emotions in positive ways.

Some people may be able to stop self-injuring on their own. They may grow out of a crisis or situation with which self-injury helped them cope. In the words of one young woman who was able to leave the toxic environment in which she was living, "I was on my own for the first time. Living my life without walking on eggshells. I started to love life. I became the happiest I've ever been. And I guess around that time I found other ways to express myself. Writing, meditation, exercise. . . . Now even the worst of news doesn't make me want to cut."[68]

For others, self-injury disappears fairly quickly once they identify and begin to deal with the underlying cause of their pain or emptiness. Still others might find that self-injury has become something they depend on and part of how they define themselves. Exploring and learning what lies behind the self-injury and addressing the larger issues can help and will take time, patience, and determination on the part of both the person seeking to recover and the therapist.

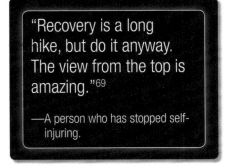

"Recovery is a long hike, but do it anyway. The view from the top is amazing."[69]

—A person who has stopped self-injuring.

A Future Beyond Self-Injury

The effectiveness of treatment for self-injury will vary, depending on the person's emotional or psychological state, the person's external situation, and the nature of any underlying mental health conditions. Reaching out for help is the first step. With treatment, there is hope for recovery. As one person who has stopped self-injuring put it, "Recovery is a long hike, but do it anyway. The view from the top is amazing."[69]

SOURCE NOTES

Introduction: The Hidden Epidemic

1. Quoted in Marilee Strong, *A Bright Red Scream: Self-Mutilation and the Language of Pain*. New York: Penguin, 2009, p. 101.

2. Quoted in Amanda Purington and Karene Booker, *Understanding Self-Injury*, Department of Human Development Outreach & Extension, Cornell University, 2011. www.human.cornell.edu.

3. Janis Whitlock and Karen Rodham, "Understanding Nonsuicidal Self-Injury in Youth," *School Psychology Forum*, Winter 2013, p. 93.

Chapter 1: What Is Self-Injury?

4. Quoted in Strong, *A Bright Red Scream*, p. 2.

5. Steven Jellá, "Self-Harm Training," lecture, Behavioral Health Education & Training Academy, Academy for Professional Excellence, San Diego State University, March 12, 2015.

6. Quoted in Strong, *A Bright Red Scream*, p. 3.

7. Vanessa Vega, *Comes the Darkness, Comes the Light: A Memoir of Cutting, Healing, and Hope*. New York: AMACOM, 2007, pp. ix–x.

8. Judy A. Stone and Shari M. Sias, "Self-Injurious Behavior: A Bi-Modal Treatment Approach to Working with Adolescent Females," *Journal of Mental Health Counseling*, July 2003, p. 117.

9. E. David Klonsky, "Non-Suicidal Self-Injury in United States Adults: Prevalence, Sociodemographics, Topography and Functions," *Psychological Medicine*, June 2011, p. 1981.

10. Andrea L. Barrocas et al., "Rates of Nonsuicidal Self-Injury in Youth: Age, Sex and Behavioral Methods in a Community Sample," *Pediatrics*, July 2012, p. 39.

11. Whitlock and Rodham, "Understanding Nonsuicidal Self-Injury in Youth," p. 95.

12. Strong, *A Bright Red Scream*, p. 18.

13. Matthew K. Nock, "Self-Injury," *Annual Review of Clinical Psychology*, April 2010, p. 347.

14. Vega, *Comes the Darkness, Comes the Light*, p. x.

15. Lindsay A. Taliaferro et al., "Factors Distinguishing Youth Who Report Self-Injurious Behavior: A Population-Based Sample," *Academic Pediatrics*, May/June 2012, p. 205.

16. Karen Conterio and Wendy Lader, *Bodily Harm: The Breakthrough Healing Program for Self-Injurers*. New York: Hyperion, 1998, p. 16.

Chapter 2: Why Do People Self-Injure?

17. Nock, "Self-Injury," p. 346.

18. Quoted in Strong, *A Bright Red Scream*, p. 32.

19. Mayo Clinic staff, "Diseases and Conditions: Self-Injury/Cutting," Mayo Foundation for Medical Education and Research, December 6, 2012. www.mayoclinic.org.

20. Strong, *A Bright Red Scream*, p. xxiii.

21. Quoted in Steven Levenkron, *Cutting: Understanding and Overcoming Self-Mutilation*. New York: Norton, 2006, p. 26.

22. Quoted in Levenkron, *Cutting*, p. 27.

23. Quoted in Strong, *A Bright Red Scream*, p. 5.

24. Personal communication with a survivor of self-injury, May 20, 2015.

25. Vega, *Comes the Darkness, Comes the Light*, p. 29.

26. Moya Alfonso and Robert F. Dedrick, "Self-Injury Among Early Adolescents," *American Journal of Health Education*, March/April 2010, p. 81.

27. Brian Daniel Smith, "Self-Mutilation and Pharmacotherapy," *Psychiatry*, October 2005, p. 31.

28. Quoted in Strong, *A Bright Red Scream*, p. 159.

29. Vega, *Comes the Darkness, Comes the Light*, pp. 63–64.

30. Nock, "Self-Injury," p. 352.

31. Quoted in BBC, "The *Panorama* Interview," transcript of interview with Princess Diana by Martin Bashir, November 1995. www.bbc.co.uk.

32. Conterio and Lader, *Bodily Harm*, p. 15.

33. Krysten, "I'll Tell You Why People Cut Themselves," HealthyPlace, 2011. www.healthyplace.com.

34. Quoted in Strong, *A Bright Red Scream*, p. 58.

Chapter 3: What Is It like to Live with Self-Injury?

35. Strong, *A Bright Red Scream*, p. xxi.

36. Vega, *Comes the Darkness, Comes the Light*, p. 1.

37. Quoted in Strong, *A Bright Red Scream*, p. 36.

38. Vega, *Comes the Darkness, Comes the Light*, p. 4.

39. Quoted in Levenkron, *Cutting*, p. 38.

40. Krysten, "I'll Tell You Why People Cut Themselves."

41. Vega, *Comes the Darkness, Comes the Light*, p. 6.

42. Quoted in Strong, *A Bright Red Scream*, p. 58.

43. Vanessa, "Stop Cutting Yourself! Here's How," HealthyPlace, January 2014. www.healthyplace.com.

44. Quoted in Strong, *A Bright Red Scream*, p. 111.

45. Levenkron, *Cutting*, p. 42.

46. Quoted in Levenkron, *Cutting*, p. 136.

47. Janis Whitlock et al., "Non-suicidal Self-Injury in a College Population: General Trends and Sex Differences," *Journal of American College Health*, August 2011, p. 695.

48. Strong, *A Bright Red Scream*, p. xxix.

49. Quoted in Strong, *A Bright Red Scream*, pp. 57–58.

50. Quoted in Strong, *A Bright Red Scream*, p. xxiv.

51. Dusty Miller, *Women Who Hurt Themselves: A Book of Hope and Understanding*. New York: Basic Books, 2005, p. x.

Chapter 4: Can Self-Injury Be Treated or Cured?

52. Stone and Sias, "Self-Injurious Behavior," p. 120.

53. Quoted in Stone and Sias, "Self-Injurious Behavior," p. 124.

54. Quoted in Strong, *A Bright Red Scream*, p. 6.

55. Patrick L. Kerr et al., "Nonsuicidal Self-Injury: A Review of Current Research for Family Medicine and Primary Care Physicians," *Journal of the American Board of Family Medicine*, March/April 2010, p. 240.

56. Barent Walsh, "Clinical Assessment of Self-Injury: A Practical Guide," *Journal of Clinical Psychology*, November 2007, p. 1,060.

57. Jennifer Muehlenkamp et al., "Interpersonal Features and Functions of Nonsuicidal Self-Injury," *Suicide and Life-Threatening Behavior*, February 2013, p. 67.

58. Walsh, "Clinical Assessment of Self-Injury," p. 1,061.

59. Quoted in Strong, *A Bright Red Scream*, p. 2.

60. Quoted in Walsh, "Clinical Assessment of Self-Injury," p. 1,060.

61. Quoted in Strong, *A Bright Red Scream*, p. 162.

62. Quoted in Strong, *A Bright Red Scream*, p. 167.

63. Walsh, "Clinical Assessment of Self-Injury," p. 1,059.

64. Levenkron, *Cutting*, pp. 199–200.

65. Stone and Sias, "Self-Injurious Behavior," p. 123.

66. Nienke Kool et al., "Behavioral Change in Patients with Severe Self-Injurious Behavior: A Patient's Perspective," *Archives of Psychiatric Nursing*, February 2009, p. 27.

67. Quoted in Strong, *A Bright Red Scream*, p. 164.

68. Personal communication with a survivor of self-injury, May 20, 2015.

69. Quoted in Purington and Booker, *Understanding Self-Injury*.

ORGANIZATIONS TO CONTACT

American Psychological Association
750 First St. NE
Washington, DC 20002
phone: (800) 374-2721 or (202) 336-5500

The American Psychological Association is the leading scientific and professional organization representing psychology in the United States. Its mission is to advance the creation, communication, and application of psychological knowledge to benefit society and improve people's lives. The website's search function can be used to find a variety of materials on self-injury.

Cornell Research Program on Self-Injury and Recovery
Beebe Hall, Cornell University
110 Plantations Rd.
Ithaca, NY 14853
phone: (607) 255-6179
e-mail: info@selfinjury.bctr.cornell.edu
website: www.selfinjury.bctr.cornell.edu

The Cornell Research Program on Self-Injury and Recovery has conducted multiple studies on a wide variety of self-injury topics and has translated the results into user-friendly materials.

LifeSIGNS (Self-Injury Guidance & Network Support)
e-mail: info@lifesigns.org.uk
website: www.lifesigns.org.uk

LifeSIGNS is an online, user-led organization based in the United Kingdom. Led by people with experience with self-injury, the group provides information and support to people affected by self-injury.

Mental Health America (MHA)

2000 N. Beauregard St., 6th Floor
Alexandria, VA 22311
phone: (800) 969-6642 or (703) 684-7722
fax: (703) 684-5968
website: www.mentalhealthamerica.net

The MHA is a community-based nonprofit dedicated to helping all Americans achieve wellness by living mentally healthier lives. Its work is driven by the commitment to promote mental health as a critical part of overall wellness, including prevention services for all, early identification and intervention for those at risk, and integrated care and treatment for those who need it, with recovery as the goal.

S.A.F.E. (Self-Abuse Finally Ends) Alternatives

10 Bergman Ct.
Forest Park, IL 60302
toll-free: (800) 366-8288
website: www.selfinjury.com

S.A.F.E. Alternatives is a nationally recognized treatment approach, professional network, and education resource base that is committed to helping people achieve an end to self-injury. It is the go-to site for many professionals and one of the earliest organizations to address self-injury.

Self Injury Foundation

PO Box 962
South Haven, MI 49090
phone: (888) 962-6774
fax: (888) 296-7988
e-mail: info@selfinjuryfoundation.org
website: www.selfinjuryfoundation.org

The Self Injury Foundation provides funding for research, advocacy, support, and education for self-injurers, their loved ones, and the professionals who work with them. The foundation provides up-to-date information and resources on self-injury.

Self-Injury Outreach and Support (SiOS)

website: http://sioutreach.org

A collaboration between McGill University and the University of Guelph, SiOS is a nonprofit international outreach organization providing current information and resources about self-injury to individuals who self-injure and those who have recovered, as well as their caregivers, families, friends, teachers, and health professionals who work with them.

Sidran Institute

PO Box 436
Brooklandville, MD 21022
phone: (410) 825-8888
fax: (410) 560-0134
website: www.sidran.org

The Sidran Institute focuses on helping people understand, recover from, and treat traumatic stress and associated disorders, including self-injuries. The institute has a wealth of materials designed for high school and college students.

Substance Abuse and Mental Health Services Administration (SAMHSA)

1 Choke Cherry Rd.
Rockville, MD 20857
phone: (877) 726-4727
website: www.samhsa.gov

SAMHSA is the agency within the US Department of Health and Human Services that leads public health efforts to advance the behavioral health of the nation. SAMHSA's mission is to reduce the impact of substance abuse and mental illness on America's communities.

FOR FURTHER RESEARCH

Books

Patricia A. Adler and Peter Adler, *The Tender Cut: Inside the Hidden World of Self-Injury*. New York: New York University Press, 2011.

Lisa Ferentz, *Letting Go of Self-Destructive Behaviors: A Workbook of Hope and Healing*. New York: Routledge, 2015.

Lori G. Plante, *Bleeding to Ease the Pain: Cutting and Self-Injury*. Lanham, MD: Rowman & Littlefield, 2010.

Chris Simpson, *Cutting and Self-Harm*. Santa Barbara, CA: Greenwood, 2015.

Marilee Strong, *A Bright Red Scream: Self-Mutilation and the Language of Pain*. New York: Penguin, 2009.

Jason J. Washburn et al., *Self-Injury: Simple Answers to Complex Questions*. Hoffman Estates, IL: Alexian Brothers, 2014.

Internet Sources

Peter Adler and Patti Adler, "Quitting Self-Injury," *Psychology Today*, February 16, 2012. www.psychologytoday.com/blog/the-deviance-society/201202/quitting-self-injury.

Melissa Healy, "Self-Injury: Even Little Boys and Girls Do It," *Los Angeles Times*, June 11, 2012. http://articles.latimes.com/2012/jun/11/news/la-heb-self-injury-kids-20120611.

Jessica Lahey, "Why Teenagers Cut, and How to Help," *Parenting* (blog), *New York Times*, October 30, 2014. http://parenting.blogs.nytimes.com/2014/10/30/why-teenagers-cut-and-how-to-help/?_r=0.

Mayo Clinic, "Self-Injury/Cutting," December 6, 2012. www.mayoclinic.org/diseases-conditions/self-injury/basics/definition/con-20025897.

MedLine Plus, "Self-Harm," May 21, 2015. www.nlm.nih.gov/med lineplus/selfharm.html.

Mental Health America, "Self-Injury." www.mentalhealthamerica .net/self-injury.

National Alliance on Mental Illness, "Self-Harm," 2015. www.nami .org/Learn-More/Mental-Health-Conditions/Related-Conditions /Self-harm.

Edward A. Selby, "Cutting to Escape from Emotional Pain?," *Overcoming Self-Sabotage* (blog), *Psychology Today*, January 30, 2010. www .psychologytoday.com/blog/overcoming-self-sabotage/201001/cu tting-escape-emotional-pain.

WebMD, "Self-Injury." www.webmd.com/depression/self-injury-dis order.

Websites

HelpGuide.org (www.helpguide.org). A nonprofit organization that gathers and disseminates information on mental health topics.

Psychology Today (www.psychologytoday.com). The online presence of the magazine *Psychology Today*, which has a number of articles on self-injury.

self-injury.net (https://self-injury.net). Led by a woman with a history of self-injury, this is a community with an extensive list of frequently asked questions about self-injury and material about resources and recovery.

INDEX

PICTURE CREDITS

ABOUT THE AUTHOR

Janice M. Yuwiler has a master's degree in public health. She has spent more than twenty years working to prevent children and adolescents from being injured and to ensure children and adults get the social or mental health services they need. Yuwiler has a background in epidemiology and molecular biology. Her other books include *Compact Research: Diabetes*, *Family Violence*, and *Great Medical Discoveries: Insulin*. Yuwiler is a native Californian who enjoys living in sunny California with her husband and three children.